Sod Gomorrah Today

Seeing the Evidence

Ana Kerner

Sodom and Gomorrah Today
Seeing the Evidence

ISBN: 1539828409
ISBN-13: 978-1539828402

Cover design by Ana Kerner.

The following were referred to for Bible quotations:

The Holy Bible in Hebrew and English, Copyright 2014 by The Bible Society in Israel.

The Scriptures, Copyright 2012 by the Institute for Scripture Research, South Africa.

Langenscheidt Pocket Hebrew Dictionary to the Old Testament, Hebrew English, by Dr. Karl Feyerabend, Printed in Germany.

The Holy Bible, Tree of Life Version, Copyright 2015 by the Messianic Jewish Family Bible Society, Grand Rapids, MI.

Holman Christian Standard Bible, Copyright 2009 by Holman Bible Publishers, Nashville, Tennessee.

You Can Buy My Books at: www.amazon.com

You Can Contact me at: annsart29@gmail.com

DEDICATION

I dedicate this book to
the Truth of the Word of God…

CONTENTS

STORY IN GENESIS

Almost everyone has heard the story about the ancient cities of Sodom and Gomorrah. And how the God of the Bible judged them for their wickedness by raining upon them burning sulfur. Thus these cities, and three others in the area, were completely destroyed.

But is this story true? Or is it and other Biblical accounts just imaginary? Are these stories made up by the men who wrote them or did they really take place? Is there any evidence of Sodom and Gomorrah today?

The Bible contains many stories that may be hard for some to believe. Most people question things that are "out of the ordinary".

Actually, I think questioning is a good thing. I like to check things out for myself too. This is what led me to studying Hebrew.

I wanted to read the Scriptures in their original language so I could really understand them. No language can be perfectly translated into another one. Things are always missed, or misinterpreted, or misunderstood in the process. Studying Hebrew has opened up a whole new understanding of Scripture for me. Hebrew has a depth that you cannot get in the English. Not only that but most Hebrew words have several meanings. This brings a richness to the Word of God and a clearer understanding that only come in the original language.

Now back to the question, is the story of Sodom and Gomorrah true?

First, I will give you the Scripture verses about the destruction of these cities. But, before I do, I want to tell you right away that if you do not have your own Bible, go out and buy one. Then start reading in it everyday. It will change your life. Maybe you go to church or synagogue now, or maybe you don't. Either way, if you are not reading the Bible for yourself you are not connected to your "Spiritual Lifeline".

OK, we will start in Genesis Chapter 13:

"Then Abram went up from Egypt to the Negev (the desert area in southern Israel) - he, his wife, and all he had, and Lot (his nephew) with him. Abram was very rich in livestock, silver, and gold...

Now Lot, who was traveling with Abram, also had flocks, herds, and tents. But the land was unable to support them as long as they stayed together, for they had so many possessions that they could not stay together, and there was quarreling between the herdsmen of Abram's livestock and the herdsmen of Lot's livestock...

Then Abram said to Lot, 'Please, let's not have quarreling between you and me, or between your herdsmen and my herdsmen, since we are relatives. Isn't the whole land before you? Separate from me: If you go to the left, I will go to the right; If you go to the right, I will go to the left.'

Lot looked out and saw that the entire Jordan Valley as far as Zoar was well watered everywhere like the LORD'S garden and the land of Egypt. This was before the LORD destroyed Sodom and Gomorrah.

So Lot chose the entire Jordan Valley for himself. Then Lot journeyed eastward, and they separated from each other. Abram lived in the land of Canaan, but Lot lived in the cities of the valley and set up his tent near Sodom.

Now the men of Sodom were evil, sinning greatly against the LORD."

Read that last line again: **"Now the men of Sodom were evil, sinning greatly against the LORD."**

This goes along with what it says in 2 Peter 2:7.

"...righteous Lot, distressed by the unrestrained behavior of the immoral (for as he lived among them, that righteous man tormented himself day by day with the lawless deeds he saw and heard)..."

According to these Biblical accounts, Sodom was a city filled with wicked people, lawless and immoral. It also tells us that Lot himself was a righteous man who lived among them. We find out in the Bible that Lot lived in Sodom for many years. It is most probable that Lot tried to influence this city to turn to God and away from it's evil practices. But we find out in Genesis 18 & 19 that, even if this was the case, Sodom remained a very wicked city.

Let's pick up the story in Genesis 18.

"Then the LORD appeared to Abraham at the oaks of Mamre while he was sitting in the entrance of his tent during the heat of the day. He looked up, and he saw three men standing near him...

He served them as they ate under the tree...

The men got up from there and looked out over Sodom,

and Abraham was walking with them to see them off.

Then the LORD said, 'Should I hide what I am about to do from Abraham? Abraham is to become a great and powerful nation, and all the nations of the earth will be blessed through him. For I have chosen him so that he will command his children and his house after him to keep the way of the LORD by doing what is right and just. This is how the LORD will fulfill to Abraham what He promised him.'

Then the LORD said, 'The outcry against Sodom and Gomorrah is immense, and their sin is extremely serious. I will go down to see if what they have done justifies the cry that has come up to Me. If not, I will find out.'

The men turned from there and went toward Sodom

while Abraham remained standing before the LORD. Abraham stepped forward and said, 'Will You really sweep away the righteous with the wicked? What if there are 50 righteous people in the city? Will You really sweep it away instead of sparing the place for the sake of the 50 righteous people who are in it? You could not possibly do such a thing, to kill the righteous with the wicked, treating the righteous and the wicked alike. You could not possibly do that! Won't the Judge of all the earth do what is just?'

The LORD said, 'If I find 50 righteous people in the city of Sodom, I will spare the whole place for their sake.'

Then Abraham answered, 'Since I have ventured to speak to the LORD – even though I am dust and ashes – suppose the 50 righteous lack five. Will you destroy the whole city for lack of five?'

He replied, 'I will not destroy it if I find 45 there.'

Then he spoke to Him again, 'Suppose 40 are found there?'

He answered, 'I will not do it on account of 40.'

Then he said, 'Let the Lord not be angry, and I will speak further. Suppose 30 are found there?'

He answered, 'I will not do it if I find 30 there.'

Then he said, 'Since I have ventured to speak to the Lord, suppose 20 are found there?'

He replied, 'I will not destroy it on account of 20.'

Then he said, 'Let the Lord not be angry, and I will speak one more time. Suppose 10 are found there?'

He answered, 'I will not destroy it on account of 10.'

When the LORD had finished speaking with Abraham, He departed, and Abraham returned to his place."

Five Chapters after we read about Lot moving to Sodom, we are told that Sodom and Gomorrah are so wicked that the cries of their victims have reached to the LORD God. Not only that, but things were so serious that He came down to investigate these cities for Himself.

Abraham (God had changed his name from Abram to Abraham) questioned God concerning the fate of these cities. Would the Judge of the earth destroy Sodom and Gomorrah if there were righteous people in these cities? What about 50 righteous, what about 10?

The LORD God assured Abraham that if He found only 10 righteous people in the city, He would hold back His judgment for their sake.

Lets see what happened in Chapter 19.

"The two angels (messengers) entered Sodom in the evening as Lot was sitting at Sodom's gate. When Lot saw them, he got up to meet them. He bowed with his face to the ground and said, 'My lords, turn aside to your servant's house, wash your feet, and spend the night. Then you can get up early and go on your way.'

'No,' they said. 'We would rather spend the night in the city square.'

But he urged them so strongly that they followed him and went into his house. He prepared a feast and baked unleavened bread for them, and they ate."

Lot, Abraham's nephew was still living in Sodom but when he saw the two angels (messengers) come into the city he was so concerned for their safety that he urged them to come to his house.

Let's continue with the story in Chapter 19.

"Before they went to bed, the men of the city of Sodom, both young and old, the whole population, surrounded the house. They called out to Lot and said, 'Where are the men who came to you tonight? '"

The story goes on and describes the wickedness of the whole city. We will pick it up in verse 15.

"At daybreak the angels (messengers) urged Lot on: 'Get up! Take your wife and your two daughters who are here, or you will be swept away in the punishment of the city.' But he hesitated. Because of the LORD's compassion for him, the men grabbed his hand, his wife's hand, and the hands of his two daughters. Then they brought him out and left him outside the city."

This is really something! Lot, even though he was a righteous man, he had a hard time leaving this wicked city. So did his wife and two daughters. The messengers from God had to actually grab their hands to get them to leave before the city was destroyed.

We are now in verse 17.

"As soon as the angels got them outside, one of them said, 'Run for your lives! Don't look back and don't stop anywhere on the plain! Run to the mountains, or you will be swept away!'

But Lot said to them, 'No, my lords – please. Your servant has indeed found favor in your sight, and you have shown me great kindness by saving my life. But I can't run to the mountains; the disaster will overtake me, and I will die. Look, this town is close enough for me to run to. It is a small place. Please let me go there – it is only a small place, isn't it? - so that I can survive.'...

The sun had risen over the land when Lot reached Zoar. Then out of the sky the LORD rained burning sulfur on Sodom and Gomorrah from the LORD. He demolished these cities, the entire plain, all the inhabitants of the cities, and whatever grew on the ground.

But his wife looked back and became a pillar of salt.

Early in the morning Abraham went to the place where he had stood before the LORD. He looked down toward Sodom and Gomorrah and all the land of the plain, and he saw that smoke was going up from the land like the smoke of a furnace. So it was, when God destroyed the cities of the plain, He remembered Abraham and brought Lot out of the middle of the upheaval when He demolished the cities where Lot had lived."

Lot and his daughters barely escaped the destruction. His wife could not resist turning back to see what was happening to the cities of Sodom and Gomorrah.

And this cost her her life.

Ana Kerner

WHERE ARE
SODOM AND GOMORRAH
LOCATED?

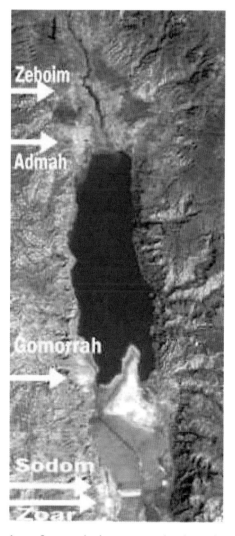

There is a lot of speculation as to the locations of Sodom and Gomorrah. Some sources put them both to the south of the Salt Sea or the Dead Sea. Some put them in the country of Jordan.

From the physical evidence, I believe this map is most accurate. We have seen for ourselves the ruins of cities in each of the locations on this map. The evidence of the city of Zeboim is just south of Jericho before you get to the Dead Sea. Not much further down Highway 90 are more ruins. This would be in the location of Admah. Gomorrah lies just beneath the ancient fortress of Masada on the side towards the Dead Sea. Sodom actually has several signs by it's location at the very southern end of the Dead Sea. Zoar is probably on the south side of the Dead Sea, just east of Sodom. The hills Lot and his family were told to flee to by the messengers was no doubt the large hills that are in the country of Jordan today. They rise up on the eastern side of the Dead Sea.

The evidence is clear. As you drive south of Jericho on Highway 90 towards the Dead Sea or Salt Sea, you see large areas of very light, almost white structural formations. They stand out from the hills and from the sand because of their contrast in color. In the early morning they can look almost orange because of the sun's reflexion on them.

These formations are obviously not made by natural means. They have many 90 degree angles, even door and window openings. Some roofs have peaks. There are evidences of towers. Some of the houses are still easily identifiable as houses even after thousands of years!

We were really amazed by what we saw. The city of Sodom was much larger than I had expected! 2 Peter 2:6 describes Sodom and Gomorrah after their destruction.

"...He reduced the cities of Sodom and Gomorrah to **ashes** and **condemned them to ruin**, making them an example to those who were going to be ungodly..."

You can see this today. In each of the locations of these cities on the map there is utter destruction. Nothing is growing there and no one is living there. They are, just as the Scripture says, ashes and ruin.

There has been archeological evidence of sulfur "balls" being found in the ruins of these cities. They are often discovered in a pattern that raindrops would make. This, once again, backs up the Biblical account of God raining burning sulfur upon the cities of the plain by the Dead Sea.

Just a note here. The fact that there is evidence today of several cities surrounding what is now known as the Dead Sea or Salt Sea shows us that there used to be fresh water here, not salt water. Why? Because all cities need a fresh water supply and as the Dead Sea is today, it is not drinkable for all the minerals it contains. Something changed this fresh source of water into what it is today. There is so much salt in the Dead Sea that it makes a person float! Just pick up your feet and you are floating in the water!

WHAT CAN WE LEARN
FROM THE DESTRUCTION
OF THESE CITIES?

Let's take a look back at the Biblical account of the destruction of Sodom, Gomorrah and the other cities of the plain.

First, why were these cities destroyed?

Several times we are told it is because of the wickedness of the people who lived there. We see this wickedness had completely overtaken the cities and the people had not turned away from doing what was evil in the eyes of God.

We are told that cries had gone up to Heaven because of their wickedness. This must be the cries of the victims. Evil always has it's victims. God gave us His instructions, the Torah, on how we are to relate to Him and to our fellowman in such ways that we will live in peace and not bring destruction upon ourselves.

When people turn away from the ways of God they actually turn to ways that will destroy them in the end. They will also destroy the people around them. This is not what God has intended for us. God wants us to live blessed lives. He wants us to have joy and prosperity along with peace. His ways bring LIFE. When we try to live apart from God's instructions to us we actually bring DEATH and DESTRUCTION.

There is a very important passage in Scripture, Deuteronomy 11:26-28.

"Look, today I set before you a blessing and a curse; there will be a blessing, if you obey the commands of the LORD your God I am giving you today, and a curse, if you do not obey the commands of the LORD your God and you turn aside from the path I command you today by following other gods you have not known..."

Often Christians are taught that "the Law has been nailed to the cross" and therefore it "does not apply to us today".

REALLY?

Isn't God "the same yesterday, today and forever"?

Isn't Y'shuah (Jesus) the Living Word of God?

Isn't the Torah (instruction) the Written Word of God?

Doesn't that make Y'shuah (Jesus) and the Torah (instruction) one and the same?

What was nailed to the cross was our debt because of our sins. NOT GOD'S INSTRUCTIONS TO US!

God gave us instructions so we could relate to Him and to other people in healthy, life giving ways. He wants us to live a blessed life. He was warning us that if we do things our way, with our limited understanding, we would fail, we would destroy not only ourselves but those around us as well. This is not what He wants for us!

We are told in 1 Corinthians 10:11 something we would do well to never forget.

"Now these things happened to them as an example, and it was written down as a warning to us – on whom the ends of the ages have come. Therefore let the one who thinks that he stands watch out that he doesn't fall."

Y'shuah (Jesus) came for many reasons. He, as the Divine contraction of the Father (YHWH) in a human body, was able to demonstrate the Father's great love for each and every one of us by taking upon Himself the punishment for our sins. In doing this He has set us free from the power of sin and death in our lives! Now we are free NOT to sin! Often people think that to sin is to live in freedom...not so. Sin is bondage. It is a trap we cannot get out of apart from the mercy and grace of God through His "Son" Y'shuah (Jesus) and the blood that He shed on our behalf.

Are YOU free from the power of sin in YOUR life?

Do you want to be set free?

First, you must realize that if you accept God's free gift of salvation (freedom from sin) in your life, your life will change forever. But it will change for the better in ways you cannot even imagine right now.

The first word that Y'shuah said in his public ministry was, "Repent!" What does that mean? In Hebrew the word translated "repent" is TESHUVAH. Teshuvah actually means "to RETURN". Therefore, to repent truly means to return to God. When we "return" to Him we are turning away from a life of sin and destruction. We are accepting His will and His ways in our lives.

But how do we know how to live for God?

This is another reason Y'shuah (Jesus) came, to demonstrate for us how to "walk out" God's instructions. This is why reading your Bible is so important. You cannot know God's ways unless you learn what they are.

So, the question remains, do YOU want to be set free from the power of sin and death in YOUR life?

It is not hard. But it takes a choice. All you have to do is to say a prayer something like this one:

Father God,

I am a sinner and I need Your forgiveness in my life. I don't want to continue to live a life of destruction. I don't want to continue to ruin my life and those around me. Please set me free from the power of sin in my life!

I turn to You now and ask for Your forgiveness. Please change me into the man (woman) of God You created me to be! I want to live the rest of my life for Your glory, not my own.

Thank You for sending Y'shuah (Jesus) to die in my place! I owe my life to You! So, I surrender myself to you now and ask that You change me from the inside out and make me into a new person.

"Create in me a clean heart, O God, and renew a right Spirit within me!"

Fill me with Your Holy Spirit! Change my thoughts and my desires so that they will conform to Yours!

I give my all to You! Thank You for saving me by the power of the blood of Y'shuah (Jesus), the promised Messiah!

Amen (May it be so!)

If you prayed this prayer, or one similar, you are NOW a new creation! The old is gone and the new has come! REJOICE! Your life is about to change in amazing ways!

Be sure to connect with God and stay connected by reading your Bible everyday. Also, find a church to connect with so you can meet people who are on the same path, the path of returning to God. Then pray, talk to God as to a friend. He is there for you and He will not leave you alone, ever.

We are not done looking at the story of Sodom and Gomorrah.

What happened to Lot?

First, when his uncle Abraham asked him to go to the right or to the left so their flocks and herds could separate from each other, his flesh led him to choose the lush green plain by Sodom.

This is an important lesson for us!

What we see with our eyes is not always what is best for us!

God had given His promises to ABRAHAM not to Lot, and yet, Abraham was willing to let Lot choose his way. Abraham's trust was in God and God alone, not in the things of this world. But Lot saw more prosperity in the lush valley than in the rocky hills.

There is a passage of Scripture in Isaiah 55:9 I want to share with you.

"For as the heavens are higher than the earth, so are My ways higher than your ways, and My thoughts than your thoughts."

God's ways are not the ways of the world. His ways are so much higher than we can even imagine. But we are human and until God, through His Spirit, enlightens our eyes we are actually blind to the ways of God. Even when we return to God and are set free from the bondage of sin in our lives, there is a process of being transformed into the man or woman God created each of us to be.

So Lot, though he was "righteous", he still had lust in his eyes for the green valley below and for his prosperity in this world. But this led to his eventual downfall.

Though he is called "righteous", he allowed his soul to be "tormented" by living in an evil environment. He did this for the sake of worldly gain. In the end he lost everything, even his wife, for she had become so attached to the worldliness of Sodom that she could not resist looking back to see it's destruction.

WARNINGS AGAINST THE WICKED
AND PROMISES FOR THE RIGHTEOUS
IN PSALMS

Psalm 1

"Blessed is the man who does not walk in the counsel of the ungodly,

and does not stand in the path of sinners, and does not sit in the seat of scoffers,

but his delight is in the instruction (Torah) of YHWH (the Lord),

and he meditates in His instructions (Torah) day and night.

For he shall be as a tree planted by the rivers of water, that yields its fruit in its season,

and whose leaf does not wither,
and whatever he does prospers.

The ungodly are not so, but are like the chaff which the wind blows away.
Therefore the ungodly shall not rise in the judgment, nor sinners in the congregation of the righteous.
For YHWH (the Lord) know the way of the righteous, but the ways of the ungodly come to nothing."

Psalm 5:4-6, 11&12

"For You are not a God who takes delight in evil, nor does wickedness dwell with You.
The boasters do not stand before Your eyes; You hate all workers of wickedness.
You destroy those speaking falsehood; YHWH (the Lord) detests a man of blood and deceit.

But I enter Your house in the greatness of Your loving kindness;
I bow myself toward Your Holy (set apart) Temple in awe of You.
O YHWH (Lord), lead me in Your righteousness because of those watching me;
Make Your way straight before my face...

Let all who take refuge in You rejoice!
Let them ever shout for joy, because Your shelter them!
And let those who love Your Name exult in You.

For You bless the righteous, O YHWH (Lord);
   You surround him with favor as with a shield."

Psalm 7:12-16

"God is a righteous judge. And He is displeased everyday, if one does not repent!

He will sharpen His sword, He bends His bow and makes it ready,

He has prepared for Himself instruments of death, He makes His arrows hot for pursuers.

See, he who is bound with wickedness, and has conceived trouble and brought forth falsehood,

who has made a pit and dug it out, he will fall into the hole he has made!

His trouble will turn back upon him,

and his wrongdoing comes down on the top of his head."

Psalm 11

"In YHWH (the Lord) I have taken refuge;
Why do you say to me, 'Flee to your mountain like a bird'?
For look! The wicked bend their bow,
they set their arrow on the string,
to shoot in darkness at the upright in heart.

When the foundations are destroyed,
what shall the righteous do?

YHWH (the Lord) is in His Holy (set apart) Temple,
the throne of YHWH (the Lord) is in the heavens.
His eyes see,
His eyelids test the sons of men.
YHWH (the Lord) tries the righteous,
but He hates the wicked and the one loving violence.
Upon the wicked He rains snares,
Fire and sulfur and a scorching wind are the portion of their cup.
For YHWH (the Lord) is righteous,
He loves righteousness; those who walk straight will see His face."

Psalm 12:3

"YHWH (the Lord) does cut off all flattering lips,
a tongue that speaks boastful words."

Psalm 14:1&2

"The fool has said in his heart,
'There is no YHWH (Lord).'
They do corruptly,
they commit abominations, none of them do good.

YHWH (the Lord) looks down from the heavens on
the sons of mankind,
to see if there is a wise one,
seeking YHWH (the Lord)."

Psalm 15

"YHWH (Lord), who can dwell in Your Tent?
Who can dwell on Your Holy (set apart) mountain?
   He who walks blamelessly,
and does righteousness,
   and speaks the truth in his heart.
He has not slandered with his tongue,
   he has not done evil to this neighbor,
nor lifted up a reproach against his friend;
   In whose eyes a reprobate one is despised,
but he honors those who fear YHWH (the Lord);
   He swears to his own hurt and does not change.
He does not loan out his money at interest,
   and does not take a bribe against the innocent.

   He who does these will never be moved."

Psalm 18:25-27

"With the merciful You show mercy;
with the blameless You show Yourself blameless;
   with the clean You show Yourself clean;
and with the crooked You show Yourself crooked.
   For You save the afflicted people,
but bring down those whose eyes are haughty."

Psalm 21:8-12

"Your hand reaches all Your enemies;
Your right hand reaches those who hate You.

You make them as a **furnace of fire** in the time of Your presence;

YHWH (the Lord) does swallow them up in His anger and **fire** does consume them.

You destroy their fruit from the earth,
and their seed from among the sons of men.

For they held out evil against You;
They devised a plot but they do not prevail.

For You make them turn their back,
when You aim with Your bowstring toward their faces."

Psalm 32:1&2

"Blessed is he whose crimes are forgiven,
whose sins are covered.
　Blessed is the man to whom YHWH (the Lord)
attributes no evil,
　　and in whose spirit is no deceit."

Psalm 37:5-17

"Commit your way to YHWH (the Lord),
and trust in Him, for He will do it.
　He shall bring forth you righteous as the light,
and your justice as the noon day.
　Rest in YHWH (the Lord), and wait patiently for Him;
Do not be disturbed because of him who prospers in his
　　way, because of the man doing wickedness.

　Hold back displeasure, and turn away from anger;
do not be disturbed, also do no evil.
　For evil-doers will be cut off,
but those who wait for YHWH (the Lord) shall inherit the
earth.

　Yet a little while and the wicked are no more;
you shall look on his place, but he is not there.
　But the meek ones shall inherit the earth,
and delight themselves in abundant peace.

　The wicked plot against the righteous,

and gnash their teeth at him.

YHWH (the Lord) laughs at him,
for He sees that their day is coming.

The wicked have drawn the sword
and have bent the bow,

to cause the poor and needy to fall,
to slay those who walk straight ahead.

But their sword will enter their own heart,
and their bows will be broken.

Better is the little of the righteous one,
than the riches of the wicked.

For the arms of the wicked will be broken,
but YHWH (the Lord) sustains the righteous."

Psalm 68:1-3

"God arises, his enemies are scattered,
and those who hate Him flee before Him!
As smoke is driven away, You drive them away;
As wax melts before the **fire**, the wicked perish before God.

But the righteous are glad, they rejoice before God, they sing with gladness!"

PUTTING IT ALL TOGETHER

There is standing evidence today to the truth of the Biblical account concerning the destruction of the ancient cities of Sodom and Gomorrah. In this book, I have shown you a few of the many pictures I took in our observations of these cities.

The question is, where will YOU end up when the time comes for the Judge of all the earth to judge YOU?

This book is here as evidence to the existence of God and the truth of His Word.

I urge you to get your life right with God before it is too late. None of us knows when the time will come for us to depart from this life and pass on into the next.

We must turn to God while we are still able.

Think about your life. Think about LIFE itself!

What is life? We are told something amazing in Matthew 16:25&26, Mark 8:35&36 and Luke 9:24&25. This message is repeated THREE times, therefore it must be very significant indeed!

"For whoever wishes to save his life shall lose it, but whoever loses his life for My sake shall save it. For what does a man profit if he gains the whole world, but destroys and loses his soul?"

The world around us tells us to get rich in the things of the world. Shopping is the most popular pastime of the majority of people in America these days. Video games take up many people's time, including our children. These electronics, along with television contribute to influencing us for evil and dulling our thinking process.

Remember what happened to Sodom and Gomorrah. The people in them "pursued the world" and look where it led them.

What is the state of YOUR soul right now?

Do YOU want to really live? What about your family?

Then turn off the TV. Put away the video games. Close your checkbook. Cancel your credit cards...

Pray the prayer I suggested to you on page 25...

Then open your Bible! Be prepared to start living as the man or woman God created you to be and you will begin to live a life of miracles!

21466357R00024

Made in the USA
Columbia, SC
17 July 2018